**ABT**

# WHEN DIPLOMACY
# FAILS

## By Cory Gunderson

## VISIT US AT
## WWW.ABDOPUB.COM

Published by ABDO & Daughters, an imprint of ABDO Publishing Company, 4940 Viking Drive, Suite 622, Edina, Minnesota 55435. Copyright ©2004 by Abdo Consulting Group, Inc. International copyrights reserved in all countries. No part of this book may be reproduced in any form without written permission from the publisher.

Printed in the United States.

Edited by: Sheila Rivera
Contributing Editors: Christopher Schafer, Paul Joseph
Graphic Design: Arturo Leyva, David Bullen
Cover Design: Castaneda Dunham, Inc.
Photos: AP/Wide World, Corbis, Department of Defense

**Library of Congress Cataloging-in-Publication Data**

Gunderson, Cory Gideon.
    When diplomacy fails / Cory Gideon Gunderson.
      p. cm.--(War in Iraq)
      Includes index.
    Summary: Describes the history of Iraq, the events during the first Gulf War in 1991, the decade of tension that followed, and the actions that led to the United States' attack on that country in 2003.
      ISBN 1-59197-502-6
      1. Iraq War, 2003--Juvenile literature. [1. Iraq--Foreign relations--United States. 2. United States--Foreign relations--Iraq. 3. Iraq War, 2003.] I. Title. II. Series.

DS79.76 .G86 2003
956.7044'3--dc21

                                                                    2003051984

# TABLE OF CONTENTS

U.S. president George W. Bush declares war on the Iraqi government on March 19, 2003.

# HISTORY OF IRAQ

When dealing with conflicts, governments can achieve their goals in a number of ways. Diplomacy and military action, on opposite ends of the spectrum, are two ways to do so. Most world citizens depend upon their governments to solve conflicts with other governments in a diplomatic way. They want their leaders to discuss differences and come to agreements that benefit all parties. Most of all, they want to avoid war.

Years of diplomatic efforts between U.S. presidents and Iraq's president Saddam Hussein failed. On March 19, 2003, President George W. Bush declared war on Saddam's government. Bush believed that the Iraqi leader was hiding weapons of mass destruction. He also considered Iraq a country that supported terrorism.

On September 11, 2001, terrorists hijacked and crashed four airplanes in the United States. Thousands of people died. After that tragedy, President Bush wasn't willing to risk further harm to the country. Bush believed that Iraq was a threat. He wanted to make sure that Saddam could not use his terrorist connections to threaten any countries.

The relationship between the United States and Iraq was not always so poor. In fact, former U.S. presidents had armed

Iraq with weapons throughout much of the 1980s. The United States and other Western nations supported Iraq through its fight with its neighbor, Iran, during that time.

So how did the diplomatic relationship between Iraq and the United States turn into a warring one? For answers to this question, we need to understand what shaped the nation of Iraq. We also need to understand how its leader, Saddam, could turn allies into enemies.

Present-day Iraq was once part of a massive region known as Mesopotamia. The word *Mesopotamia* means the Land Between the Rivers. The Tigris and Euphrates Rivers flowed through Mesopotamia and created a fertile plain. This area has been called the Fertile Crescent. The people of Mesopotamia benefited from the fertile land and the ample supply of water. Cultures such as the Assyrian, Babylonian, Parthian, and Sumerian flourished in this region for centuries.

Mesopotamia has also been called the cradle of civilization because so much of civilization was born there. About 10,000 years ago, animals and plants were domesticated in this area. This means that man began to control plants and animals to benefit people. Money was invented there almost 5,000 years ago. The plow, the wheel, and writing also originated there.

The Islamic religion spread through this area in the seventh century, shortly after the death of the prophet Muhammad. Muhammad was the religion's founder. During the eighth century, Baghdad became the capital of this Islamic-ruled land.

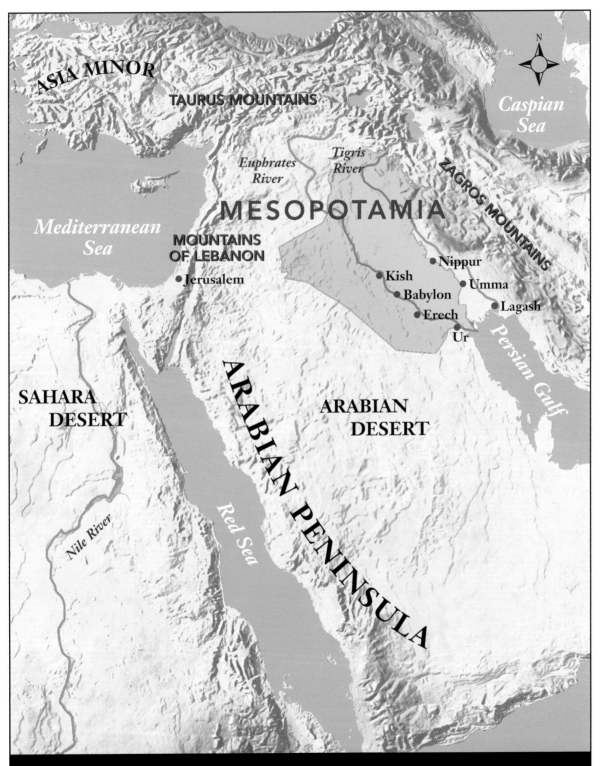

Map of Mesopotamia with modern-day Iraq highlighted

In the sixteenth century, Mesopotamia was taken over by the Ottoman Empire. The Ottoman Turks divided the land into three sections: Mosul, Baghdad, and Basra. The Turks controlled this territory until the early twentieth century.

In 1914, near the start of World War I, the sultan of the Ottoman Empire declared a holy war, or jihad. He declared France, Russia, and the United Kingdom as the empire's enemies. The sultan hoped that by partnering with Germany in this conflict his empire could regain land it had lost in previous wars.

In 1917, British forces invaded Mesopotamia to protect British oil interests. The British navy depended upon the region's oil to fuel its equipment. The British Empire also wanted to show its power in the region. It took control of Baghdad, and the Ottoman Empire collapsed. The United Kingdom then became the dominant force in this region.

The British government had promised independence to the Arabs it now controlled. Instead, the League of Nations declared the Arab land of Iraq a "mandate territory" in 1920. This meant that the British Empire would supervise the area and help it prepare for independence. The Arabs did not accept the British supervision as help. They reacted in anger. They felt betrayed that they were not given the full independence promised them.

Under the League of Nations mandate, the Iraqi borders that exist today were established. British leaders, including Winston Churchill, set them. The country became a mixture of three very different ethnic and religious groups. The group

located in the central section of Iraq around Baghdad was made up of mostly Sunni Muslims. They controlled the country. The Kurds who lived in the north had no desire to be controlled by Baghdad. The Shiite Muslims and tribesmen who lived in the south resisted this control, too.

Iraqi resentment of the United Kingdom took root at this time. The Iraqis thought that the British purposely forced three feuding groups to try to live as one country. This unstable situation, the Arabs believed, would keep Iraq from gaining strength and unity. This would make it much easier to be controlled by outsiders, such as the United Kingdom.

The British decision to make Kuwait an independent country caused further Iraqi resentment. Iraqis believed that Kuwait's land should have been included in Iraqi territory. The creation of the separate country of Kuwait left Iraq with limited access to the Persian Gulf. In the desert land of the Middle East, access to waterways is important.

In 1921, the British government brought in King Faisal from the Hijaz region of Arabia to rule Iraq. He was to establish a monarchy in the country. Ninety-six percent of Iraqis voted to accept Faisal as their leader, even though he was an outsider. King Faisal's name was the only one the British government placed on the ballot.

Finally, in 1932, the British government agreed to allow Iraq its freedom. The Iraqis still felt controlled by the British government. The United Kingdom kept military bases in the country and insisted on training the Iraqi military. King Faisal died in 1933. Monarchs continued to rule Iraq until 1958.

King Faisal II of Iraq addresses his people in Baghdad on May 2, 1953.

In 1958, General Abdul Kassem led a successful coup against the monarchy. A coup is a military takeover of control. King Faisal II, Iraq's last king, was killed. Iraq declared itself a republic, free from British control. The coup's leaders wanted to eliminate outside control of the country. They also wanted to rid Arab lands of non-Muslims. Another goal was to change the Iraqi borders between its neighboring countries, especially Iran and Kuwait.

Saddam Hussein, a member of the Baath party, was part of a group that tried to kill Kassem in 1959. The Baath party wanted to unite Arabs. It wanted to keep control of the country out of foreign hands. It also believed in a form of socialism. Saddam had to leave Iraq after the attempt failed.

Kuwait had gained its own independence from the United Kingdom by 1961. Iraqi leader Kassem had plans to make Kuwait part of Iraq through military force. Kassem's takeover failed, and he was overthrown. Iraq agreed to recognize Kuwait's independence.

In 1968, President Ahmed Hassan al-Bakr of the Baath party was in power. With his party in control of Iraq, Saddam went back to his home country. He served as vice president and head of security. Saddam seized power in Iraq in 1979 when al-Bakr resigned.

Saddam wasted no time in trying to expand his base of power. In 1979, Islamic fundamentalists overthrew Iran's leadership. They pushed to make Iran an Islamic republic. With political unrest in Iran, Saddam saw opportunity.

In September 1980, Saddam sent troops into Iran. Iraq battled for control of Iran for eight years. Western nations such as Germany, France, the United Kingdom, and the United States supported the Iraqi government. The Western nations hoped that the Iraqi government might prevent the spread of Islamic fundamentalism. The Western countries helped the Iraqi regime develop weapons.

By 1988, Iran had suffered great losses. The threat of facing Iraq's weapons of mass destruction, such as poison gas, was too great. Both countries agreed to a United Nations (UN) peace treaty. Eight years of war with Iran had made Iraq a major power in the area. It also left the Iraqi economy in ruins.

Saddam had aggressive goals. He wanted to force the U.S. presence from the Middle East. He also wanted to return the country of Israel to Arab control. These goals required great sums of money. He saw his next opportunity in Iraq's oil-rich neighbor, Kuwait.

On August 2, 1990, the Iraqi military invaded Kuwait. The Iraqi government annexed Kuwait. This meant that the Iraqi government considered the country of Kuwait part of Iraq. The world was stunned. Countries that once considered Saddam an ally, such as the United States, now considered him an outcast. He was a ruler who couldn't be trusted. He had great potential to cause harm with weapons supplied by those who were now his enemy.

# THE UNITED NATIONS STEPS IN

The very day Iraq invaded Kuwait, the UN Security Council issued Resolution 660. This resolution condemned the Iraqi invasion.

The United Nations (UN) became an official peace-promoting organization on October 24, 1945. Its goal was much like that of the League of Nations. The purpose of both organizations was to preserve world peace through cooperation between nations. The League of Nations, which began in 1919, was unable to prevent World War II. It ceased to exist in 1946 and was replaced with the UN.

Today, 191 countries are members of the UN. That number represents most nations of the world. The UN Charter, or agreement, is accepted by all member nations. This charter explains the four purposes of the UN. Its first purpose is to maintain peace and security across nations. Its second purpose is to develop friendly relationships between nations. Helping solve problems between nations is the UN's third purpose. Its fourth purpose is to be a center for peacefully blending the actions of nations.

The UN does not make laws. It was created to help resolve conflict between nations. Nations in the UN are able

The UN Security Council works to prevent a U.S.–led invasion of Iraq.

to introduce resolutions. Each nation votes on decisions made by the UN General Assembly. No matter what the size or wealth of the country, each gets one vote.

Six groups make up the UN. They are the International Court of Justice, General Assembly, Trusteeship Council, Economic and Social Council, Secretariat, and Security Council. The Security Council played an important role in trying to prevent a U.S.-led invasion of Iraq.

The Security Council's primary role is to maintain international security and peace. Whenever there is a threat to peace, the council may gather. The UN Charter states that all member nations must follow the Security Council's decisions. Threats to peace are brought before the council. The council's first goal is to help the parties settle their issues peacefully. When this is not possible, the council works to bring the fighting to an end as quickly as possible.

Representatives from 15 member nations make up this council. Five nations are permanent members. These are China, France, Russia, the United Kingdom, and the United States. The other 10 are elected by the General Assembly. They serve two-year terms. It takes nine yes votes to make a decision formal. With few exceptions, no decision can be made if even one permanent member nation votes no.

The Security Council can take steps to ensure its decisions are carried out. It can call for economic sanctions, where a country is charged a financial penalty. The council can also call for a ban on what the country trades. This is called an embargo. It penalizes a country by restricting the amount of

money it makes from trading. On rare occasions, the council will tell a member nation it has the right to use "all necessary means" to resolve a dispute. This could include military action.

The role of the Department of Peacekeeping Operations is to help member countries and the UN secretary general maintain world peace and security. This department operates under the supervision of the Security Council and the General Assembly. It is under the command of the UN secretary general. It aids the Security Council by planning, preparing, managing, and directing UN peacekeeping initiatives.

The UN peacekeeping forces complete different tasks depending on each situation's needs. All tasks are meant to lessen human suffering and create conditions and institutions that will allow for long-lasting peace. The department also works to lessen the risks of harm that the peacekeepers face. Armed or unarmed military peacekeepers and civilians may help with peacekeeping initiatives.

These forces may be sent out to prevent boundary disputes between two groups. They may help negotiate cease-fires, where each side is told to stop fighting. They may also be sent into a country to stabilize a situation after a cease-fire has been reached. Peacekeepers may also help implement peace treaties and help governments get established.

UN Resolution 660 condemned Iraq's invasion of Kuwait. It demanded that Iraqi forces withdraw from Kuwait immediately. The Iraqi government was also ordered to begin negotiations immediately with Kuwaiti leaders to reach a peaceful agreement.

When the Iraqi government failed to implement Resolution 660, the UN issued Resolution 661. On August 6, 1990, the UN Security Council imposed economic sanctions on Iraq. The economic sanctions blocked all trading with Iraq. No funds could be transferred to the Iraqi government. Only goods and funds used for medical and humanitarian reasons were allowed. Again, Saddam and his government ignored the resolution.

On November 29, the UN responded again to Saddam's refusal to cooperate with Resolution 660. This time it issued Resolution 678. It stated that Iraqi forces had to leave Kuwait and comply with Resolution 660 by January 15, 1991. The resolution granted "member states cooperating with the government of Kuwait" permission to use all necessary means to deal with Saddam if he did not comply.

Saddam once again refused to withdraw from Kuwait. Former U.S. president George H.W. Bush led a coalition of 32 nations united to free Kuwait. On January 18, 1991, Operation Desert Storm was launched. For five weeks, the coalition forces staged a massive air war, bombing Iraqi targets and military forces. Coalition ground forces invaded Kuwait and southern Iraq on February 24. It took only four days to defeat the Iraqi ground forces and free Kuwait. On February 28, President Bush declared a cease-fire. Although Kuwait was free, Saddam remained in power in Iraq.

Many nations feared that Saddam would use biological, chemical, and nuclear weapons against future enemies. On

Former U.S. president George H.W. Bush led a coalition to free Kuwait from Iraqi control.

April 3, 1991, the UN Security Council issued Resolution 687. This called for Iraq to allow for the removal or destruction of all its weapons of mass destruction. It also forbid Iraq to create such weapons ever again. Under pressure from other countries, the Iraqi government reluctantly agreed to the UN resolution.

The UN Security Council established the United Nations Special Commission (UNSCOM). Members of UNSCOM were citizens of various nations. Their purpose was to inspect Iraq for weapons of mass destruction. These weapons were then to be removed and destroyed. UNSCOM was to prevent Iraqi facilities from making weapons, too. Members of UNSCOM were directed to work with the International Atomic Energy Agency (IAEA). Members of the IAEA, created by the UN, would focus on finding and destroying nuclear weapons. UNSCOM members were to search for chemical and biological weapons.

To encourage Saddam's cooperation, the UN said it would lift sanctions against Iraq if the country cooperated fully with weapons inspectors. As time would tell, this was not enough to secure Saddam's compliance.

Iraqi deputy foreign minister Tariq Aziz

# DECADE OF TENSION

In November 1992, Iraqi deputy foreign minister Tariq Aziz spoke to the UN Security Council. He criticized Resolution 687 and said that Iraq was in full compliance. He said that the country had no weapons of mass destruction.

The Iraqi government maintained that the inspections were part of a plan designed to continue sanctions against Iraq. Iraqi government officials began to get in the way of the UN weapons inspectors. Officials radioed ahead to warn other Iraqis of upcoming inspections. Iraqis failed to cooperate with the inspectors' requests. They were purposely vague when inspectors asked the Iraqis to allow them access to certain buildings.

The UN saw these Iraqi actions as evidence that the government was hiding banned weapons. The UN continued the weapons inspections and sanctions against Iraq. Many innocent Iraqi citizens suffered because of the UN sanctions. Many were sick and hungry. According to former UN worker Denis Halliday, who helped the Iraqi citizens, the impact of the sanctions was severe. In January 1997, Halliday said, "The [Iraqi] economy is a total disaster . . . The buildings are falling down. Twenty-five percent of the kids are not going to school anymore because they are out making money to support the family. The whole social structure is crumbling."

Saddam is said to have paraded foreign visitors past the suffering Iraqi citizens. He showed visitors empty hospital shelves. He did this to tell the world that the UN sanctions were too harsh. As Iraqi citizens were struggling to survive, Saddam built palace after palace for his own comfort.

Some of Saddam's enemies in Iraq reported that Saddam ordered the killing of one of his palace architects. This man designed and helped supervise palace building projects. The man's crime was that he described to friends the lavishness of Saddam's palaces. It is said that Saddam then had pamphlets sent to palace workers. These notices warned of the harshest punishment for those who talked about the presidential homes. These workers were not allowed to tell anyone about Saddam's excesses.

Saddam even had his own lakeside resort. This resort, named Saddamiat al Tharthar, is located about 85 miles (137 km) west of Baghdad. It contains stadiums, hospitals, parks, 625 homes, and an amusement park. Only Iraqi government officials are welcome at this resort. U.S. government officials believe that Saddam paid for the building of his empire by secretly selling oil to his supporters.

It is estimated that he spent billions of dollars to build as many as 57 palaces for himself. These presidential homes are said to have golden plumbing, European marble, and crystal chandeliers in them. The land around Saddam's palaces is said to be adorned by beautiful gardens and man-made waterfalls.

The entrance to Saddam Hussein's lakeside resort, Saddamiat al Tharthar

The gardens and waterfalls require large amounts of water. The gardens thrive while the local people don't have enough water for daily use.

On April 5, 1991, the UN Security Council issued Resolution 688. It demanded that the Iraqi government stop holding its people down. This especially applied to the Kurds who lived in northern Iraq. Saddam's government was also to allow international humanitarian organizations into Iraq. These organizations represented nations around the world. Their members were to bring food and help to the Iraqi citizens in need.

The UN saw how the Iraqi people suffered as a result of its sanctions on the Iraqi government. The Security Council issued Resolution 986 on April 14, 1995, to help the needy Iraqis. The resolution allowed countries to buy oil from Iraq. The money from oil sales was to go into an account that the UN would manage. This money would then be used to pay for food and supplies needed by the Iraqi citizens. The UN had offered Saddam the Oil-for-Food program in 1991. Saddam rejected it from 1991 until 1996. The first deliveries of food and supplies under this program did not arrive in Iraq until 1997.

Former U.S. president George H.W. Bush visited Kuwait in April 1993. He was there to celebrate the victory over Iraq in the Persian Gulf War two years earlier. While Bush was in Kuwait, the Iraqi Intelligence Service (IIS) ordered his death. Kuwaiti officials learned of the plot and were able to prevent it. Two Iraqi citizens were charged with leading a group of 16.

The group planted a bomb under the vehicle in which Bush was to travel. In June 1993, U.S. president Bill Clinton punished the Iraqi government for the plot to kill Bush. He ordered a cruise missile strike on the IIS building in Baghdad.

In October 1994, the Iraqi government began to build military forces on the Iraqi-Kuwaiti border. It also threatened to stop cooperating with the UN inspectors. In response to these threats, the U.S. government sent its military troops to the region. Iraqi leaders backed down. By November 10, 1994, Iraq's National Assembly had officially recognized Kuwait's independence.

Conflict between Iraq and the United States flared again in 1997. In early June, Iraqi officials banned U.S. weapons inspectors who were part of the UN inspections team from entering certain sites. The Iraqi government gave all U.S. inspectors a 24-hour deadline to leave the country. UN Secretary-General Kofi Annan sent three messengers to Iraq. Their role was to convince Saddam to withdraw his demand. By the end of November, the Iraqi government did reverse its decision.

In early 1998, the Iraqi government declared it would ban UNSCOM inspections. Iraqi officials said that there was an imbalance of inspectors from the United States and the United Kingdom. The UN secretary-general was able to get Iraqi officials to again back down from their threat.

At about this same time, a group of conservative U.S. citizens sent a letter to President Clinton. These citizens were worried about Iraq's threat to world security. They formed an

U.S. troops board a plane in preparation for Operation Desert Fox.

organization called the Project for a New American Century. Part of their letter said, "The only acceptable [U.S.] strategy is one that eliminates the possibility that Iraq will be able to use or threaten to use weapons of mass destruction. In the near term, this means a willingness to undertake military action as diplomacy is clearly failing. In the long term, it means removing Saddam Hussein from power."

By the end of 1998, Saddam had stopped cooperating with inspectors. The governments of the United States and the United Kingdom responded to Iraq's lack of cooperation. The two allies launched a missile attack on Iraq on December 16, 1998. This attack was called Operation Desert Fox. The goal of the operation was to "strike military and security targets in Iraq that contribute to Iraq's ability to produce, store, maintain and deliver weapons of mass destruction." Saddam's weapons program was crippled, but he remained in power.

In late 1999, more than a year after inspectors left Iraq, the UN had replaced UNSCOM with UNMOVIC. The full name of this team is the UN Monitoring Verification and Inspection Commission. Besides establishing UNMOVIC, UN Resolution 1284 also demanded full cooperation from the Iraqi government in the inspections. It also expanded the Oil-for-Food program. The Iraqi government could sell as much oil as it wanted. Officials had to agree, though, that the money earned went to buy food and medical supplies for its citizens. This resolution also called on the Iraqi government to quickly help its needy citizens.

At different times, UNMOVIC and UNSCOM were both in charge of Iraqi weapons inspections. UNMOVIC was different in that its inspectors had more power to do their jobs. UNMOVIC inspectors did not need to give Iraqi officials advanced warning of the inspection locations. The inspectors could look wherever they wanted, whenever they wanted. They could also arrange for Iraqi people to be moved to safety outside of Iraq. This would allow the Iraqi citizens to provide information without fear of Saddam's punishment.

The Iraqi government was not fully cooperative. In April 2001, the United States and the United Kingdom bombed Iraq. They struck Iraq's radar system to punish the Iraqi military for targeting the coalition's aircraft. The coalition's aircraft patrolled certain parts of the Iraqi airspace to monitor its activities.

U.S.-Iraqi tension continued. Terrorist attacks on the United States only a few months later would challenge the relationship further.

Coalition aircraft patrol Iraqi airspace.

# BUSH DECLARES WAR ON TERRORISM

On September 11, 2001, terrorists attacked the United States. They flew hijacked airplanes into both World Trade Center towers. Another slammed into the Pentagon outside Washington, D.C. A fourth crashed into a Pennsylvanian field. The terrorists used U.S. airliners, loaded with fuel, as powerful bombs. More than 3,000 innocent people lost their lives in the worst acts of terrorism the United States had ever seen.

U.S. president George W. Bush addressed the nation that evening. He promised to "find those responsible and bring them to justice." He also warned that the United States would punish those who allowed terrorists to live in their countries. He said the country would "make no distinction between the terrorists who committed these acts and those who harbor them."

By September 13, 2001, Secretary of State Colin Powell listed Osama bin Laden as the prime suspect in the attacks. Saudi-born bin Laden had inherited millions of dollars when his father died. He used his money to finance al-Qaeda, a

radical Islamic fundamentalist group. Its members resent Western influence in the world and use terrorism against Western interests.

In his September 20, 2001, address to the American people, Bush declared the U.S. War on Terrorism. "We will direct every resource at our command—every means of diplomacy, every tool of intelligence, every instrument of law enforcement, every financial influence, and every necessary weapon of war—to the disruption and to the defeat of the global terror network."

Members of the Bush administration believed that the Iraqi government had supported al-Qaeda in the past. They believed that al-Qaeda terrorists felt safe operating out of Iraq. Saddam's poor relationship with the U.S. government and his history of producing weapons of mass destruction concerned Bush and his advisers. They feared that Saddam would supply the terrorists with weapons that could cause the United States more harm. Saddam's regime had become a target of the war on terror.

The UN Security Council demanded that Saddam prove to the world that Iraq had no weapons of mass destruction. On September 17, 2002, the Iraqi government agreed to allow UN weapons inspectors back inside its country. The UN hoped that this diplomatic effort would head off a military conflict between Iraq and the United States.

UN weapons inspectors in Iraq

Bush warned that if diplomacy failed, Saddam and his government would face serious consequences. "The purposes of the United States should not be doubted. The Security Council resolutions will be enforced—the just demands of peace and security will be met—or action will be unavoidable. And a regime that has lost its legitimacy [lawfulness] will also lose its power."

U.S. president George W. Bush warns the Iraqi government.

# BUSH SEEKS UN SUPPORT

The U.S. House and Senate supported President Bush in his demand that Iraq disarm. In October 2002, Congress approved a resolution that gave Bush added power. The resolution authorized the president to use military force against Saddam's regime if it did not fully disarm.

The next month the UN Security Council adopted Resolution 1441. It demanded that the UNMOVIC inspectors have open access in Iraq to do their work. Saddam's regime also had to list all weapons of mass destruction it owned. This list was to be forwarded to the UN. The resolution warned of serious consequences if Saddam did not follow the resolution. It gave Saddam "a final opportunity to comply with disarmament obligations."

Since March 1, 2000, Hans Blix had served as the executive chairman of UNMOVIC. He led the weapons inspection efforts in Iraq. Blix was born in Sweden. From 1961 until 1981, he was a member of Sweden's UN delegation. From 1981 until 1997, he served as the director general of the IAEA.

Blix met with the UN Security Council on March 7, 2003. He reported that Iraq was in possession of al-Samoud 2 missiles.

Hans Blix, executive chairman of UNMOVIC

These missiles had the potential to travel farther than the UN allowed. Blix told the Security Council that Iraqi officials had started to destroy these weapons. He also told the council that inspectors had not found any underground or mobile weapon sites. Blix asked that Iraq be given more time to disarm completely.

The U.S. and British governments did not want to give Saddam more time. The Bush administration worried that Saddam would use the extra time to make people believe he was complying. Bush and British prime minister Tony Blair argued that the UN should enforce its resolutions regarding Iraq. They were convinced Saddam was a threat to world peace and needed to be stopped. They were the only two permanent members of the council to call on the UN Security Council to back up its resolutions with military force if Saddam did not comply by a certain date.

The three other permanent members of the council, France, Russia, and China, wanted to give Iraq more time. As permanent members of the council, they had the right to veto, or reject, resolutions. France, especially, indicated that it would veto any resolution that authorized the use of force in Iraq. Two nonpermanent council members, Germany and Syria, said they, too, would vote against the use of force.

An emergency meeting was held in the Azores on March 16, 2003. The Azores are islands in the northern Atlantic Ocean, west of mainland Portugal. Portuguese prime minister Jose Manuel Durao Barroso hosted the meeting. Bush, Blair, and Spanish prime minister José María Aznar attended.

Their work for the day was to decide how they would move forward with regard to Iraq. Aboard Air Force One that same day, White House spokesman Ari Fleischer warned, "Make no mistake, diplomacy is coming to a conclusion."

During the Azores meeting, reporters asked Bush, Blair, Barroso, and Aznar questions. Blair shared his frustrations regarding the diplomatic efforts he and other leaders had attempted. ". . . When people say haven't we exhausted all the diplomatic avenues, we tried exhausting. But understand from our perspective and from the perspective of the security of the world, we cannot simply go back to the Security Council, for this discussion to be superseded [or replaced] by that discussion, to be superseded by another discussion. That's what's happened for 12 years. That's why [Saddam's] still got the weapons of mass destruction. We have to come to the point of decision."

British prime minister Tony Blair, U.S. president George W. Bush, and Portuguese prime minister Jose Manuel Durao Barroso in the Azores

# 48-HOUR WARNING

President Bush and the leaders who met in the Azores had come to a definite decision. They decided to disarm Iraq by force without UN approval or support. Bush addressed the nation on March 17, 2003. To satisfy the U.S. allies who wanted to give Saddam more time, Bush gave Saddam a deadline. He announced, "All the decades of deceit and cruelty have now reached an end. Saddam Hussein and his sons must leave Iraq within 48 hours. Their refusal to do so will result in military conflict, commenced at a time of our choosing."

Bush also said that, "The United States, with other countries, will work to advance liberty and peace in that region." Those other countries were called the Coalition of the Willing. Within a couple days of Bush's speech, the United States had named 30 countries that were prepared to stand by it as it took action against Saddam. By late March, the coalition grew to 49.

The White House issued a statement that said, "All Coalition member nations understand the threat Saddam Hussein's weapons pose to the world and the devastation his regime has wreaked on the Iraqi people."

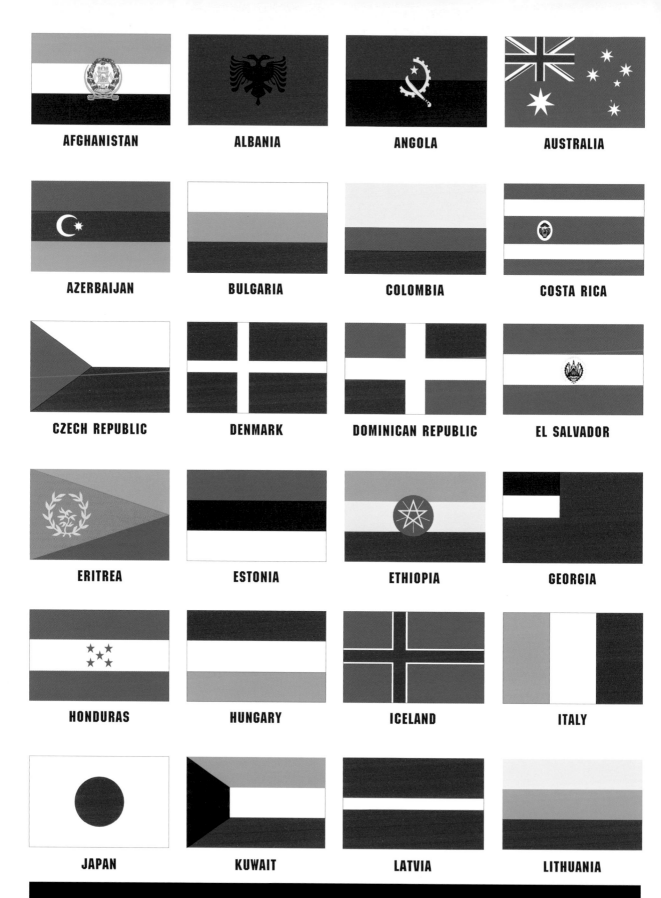

**AFGHANISTAN**

**ALBANIA**

**ANGOLA**

**AUSTRALIA**

**AZERBAIJAN**

**BULGARIA**

**COLOMBIA**

**COSTA RICA**

**CZECH REPUBLIC**

**DENMARK**

**DOMINICAN REPUBLIC**

**EL SALVADOR**

**ERITREA**

**ESTONIA**

**ETHIOPIA**

**GEORGIA**

**HONDURAS**

**HUNGARY**

**ICELAND**

**ITALY**

**JAPAN**

**KUWAIT**

**LATVIA**

**LITHUANIA**

These flags represent the countries that joined the United States in the Coalition of the Willing.

**MACEDONIA**

**MARSHALL ISLANDS**

**MICRONESIA**

**MONGOLIA**

**NETHERLANDS**

**NICARAGUA**

**PALAU**

**PANAMA**

**PHILIPPINES**

**POLAND**

**PORTUGAL**

**ROMANIA**

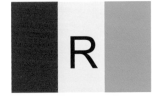

**RWANDA**

**SINGAPORE**

**SLOVAKIA**

**SOLOMON ISLANDS**

**SOUTH KOREA**

**SPAIN**

**TONGA**

**TURKEY**

**UGANDA**

**UKRAINE**

**UNITED KINGDOM**

**UZBEKISTAN**

Saddam and his sons refused to leave Iraq. An Iraqi state television announcer read a statement shortly after Bush's threat. The message read, "Iraq doesn't choose its path through foreigners and doesn't choose its leaders by decree from Washington, London, or Tel Aviv."

President Bush responded by warning that an attack on Iraq was unavoidable. The UN ordered its weapons inspectors to leave Iraq. On March 19, 2003, coalition forces launched their attack on the Iraqi government. Diplomacy had officially failed.

Shortly after President Bush announced the war with Iraq was official, U.S. task forces advanced into Iraq to launch an attack.

# WEB SITES
## WWW.ABDOPUB.COM

To learn more about diplomacy, visit ABDO Publishing Company on the World Wide Web at **www.abdopub.com**. Web sites about diplomacy are featured on our Book Links page. These links are routinely monitored and updated to provide the most current information available.

Iraqi citizens gather around Iraqi president Saddam Hussein.

# TIMELINE

**1917**

British forces invaded Mesopotamia

**1920**

League of Nations declared Iraq a British "mandate territory"

**1932**

The British gave Iraq its freedom

**1959**

Saddam had to leave Iraq after Baath party failed in coup attempt

**1968–1979**

Saddam served in the Iraqi government under President Ahmed Hassan al-Bal

**1979**

Saddam seized power in Iraq

**1980–1988**

Iraq battled its neighbor, Iran

**1990**

Iraq invaded Kuwait
UN Security Council imposed sanctions on Iraq

## 1991
Operation Desert Storm began Persian Gulf War

## 2001
September 11: More than 3,000 people killed in terrorist attacks
September 20: U.S. president George W. Bush declared War on Terrorism

## OCTOBER 2002
U.S. Congress authorized Bush to use military force against Saddam's regime

## NOVEMBER 2002
UN Security Council adopted Resolution 1441

## MARCH 16, 2003
Bush and leaders of the United Kingdom, Spain, and Portugal met in Azores

## MARCH 17, 2003
Bush gave Saddam and his sons 48 hours to leave Iraq

## MARCH 19, 2003
U.S.-led coalition launched attack on Iraq after diplomacy failed

# FAST FACTS

- Diplomacy and military action are two choices a government has to achieve its goals when dealing with conflict.

- Iraq was once part of the region known as Mesopotamia.

- British leaders created the modern country of Iraq by grouping three separate territories together. These three territories were made up of different cultures and religions.

- The United States and other Western nations supported Saddam Hussein in his war against Iran in the 1980s.

- The UN worked to prevent a U.S.-led war against Iraq.

- The UN Security Council issued many resolutions that were to rid Iraq of its weapons of mass destruction. None were fully effective.

- U.S. president George W. Bush believed that the Iraqi government supported the terrorist group al-Qaeda.

- Hans Blix, executive chairman of UNMOVIC, reported that Iraq was in possession of illegal missiles. He wanted to give Iraq additional time to disarm.

- The five permanent members of the UN Security Council disagreed on how to deal with Iraq. The United States and the United Kingdom wanted to use military force to disarm Iraq. France, Russia, and China wanted to give UN weapons inspectors more time to search Iraq.

- The United States led a Coalition of the Willing that launched an attack on Saddam's regime on March 19, 2003.

# GLOSSARY

**humanitarian:**
One concerned with the general welfare of human beings.

**Islamic fundamentalist:**
A follower of the Islamic religion who holds a strict religious point of view.

**Kurds:**
An ethnic group found in northern Iraq.

**negotiate:**
To settle an issue through discussion.

**outcast:**
One who is unacceptable to others.

**regime:**
A government in power.

**Shiite Muslim:**
A member of the branch of Islam that regards Ali and his descendants as the rightful successors to the prophet Muhammad.

**sultan:**
A ruler in certain Muslim countries.

**Sunni Muslim:**
A member of the branch of Islam that originally voted for the prophet Muhammad's successor.

**Western nation:**
A nation in the Western Hemisphere that typically has a high Christian population.

# INDEX